Janie Chase Michaels

A natural sequence :

A story of Phoenix, Arizona

Janie Chase Michaels

A natural sequence :
A story of Phoenix, Arizona

ISBN/EAN: 9783744748735

Printed in Europe, USA, Canada, Australia, Japan

Cover: Foto ©Andreas Hilbeck / pixelio.de

More available books at **www.hansebooks.com**

A NATURAL SEQUENCE.

A STORY

OF

PHOENIX, ARIZONA.

.

BY

JANIE CHASE MICHAELS.

Bangor, Maine:
Charles H. Glass & Company,
1895.

QUOTATIONS.

CHAPTER I.

" In to-day already walks to-morrow."

CHAPTER II.

"Those about her,
From her shall learn the perfect ways of honor."

CHAPTER III.

"O, for a beaker full of the warm South !"

CHAPTER IV.

"And though he trip and fall,
He shall not blind his soul with clay."

CHAPTER V.

" The secret of success is constancy to purpose."

CHAPTER VI.

"And, after all, what is a lie ?   'Tis but the truth in masquerade."

CHAPTER VII.

" Truth is the highest thing that man may keep."

A Natural Sequence.

CHAPTER I.

" In to day already walks to morrow."

THE annual rainfall usually occurs in December. But in this month of the year 189— anxious watchers searched the sky in vain for the white, fleecy specks that always herald the coming of the storm-clouds. On the ranges the cattle were dying for lack of food and water; while thick coats of dingy gray covered the green of cultivated tracts. All the Salt River Valley lay athirst beneath the scorching rays of a semi-tropical sun.

It was not until the following February that the storm elements triumphantly trailed their black skirts across the encircling mountains. As if by magic, the foot-hills became covered with a juicy grass; the desert no longer held up haggard and imploring hands of scanty vegetation; and the fruit groves and orchards became "huge seas of verdure."

Within the city, forming the commercial centre of this hot plateau, the floating particles of dust had found their proper level. Each atom seemed a magnet. Collectively, they were a good illustration of the ancient proverb, "In union there is strength." Whatever came in contact with their cohesive, adhesive surfaces was drawn with an almost irresistible force towards mother-earth. On the morning of the tenth day

of rainfall, there were not many pedes-
trians abroad. Only necessity took one
out of doors where over-shoes were almost
sure to part company with their proper
companions and attach themselves to the
black *adobe*.

Elsa Walton stood at the front window
of a house on Washington street and
gazed frowningly upon the gloomy landscape. The dwelling, modern in style
and constructed of brick, stood upon a
raised lawn, across which a graveled
path led from the front door to the
side-walk. The water ran off this beaten
way into irrigating canals dug on each
side of it. There was nothing here to
justify the two little lines gradually
deepening between the girl's eyebrows.

Beyond the fence enclosing this house,
there lay a watery sheet of no mean
dimensions. The land here sloped from

the north; and the "ditch" between side-walk and road-level had overflowed its banks. How to get around this miniature pond was a vexatious problem.

It was this perplexity that had clouded the usually pleasant face of Miss Walton. She was a teacher in the "Number One" school building; and, in spite of the storm and bad condition of the roads, must go to her post of duty. In fair weather, it was not more than a ten minutes' walk to the school-house; but now not less than half an hour would be required to reach it.

After watching for a few minutes the circling wavelets made by the pelting rain-drops, she turned away, saying: "Well! as I must test the depth of the water, I may as well be getting ready to sally forth. How I do dislike, though,

to exchange this coziness and comfort for
the outside wet and gloom."

The apartment in which she stood
revealed a girl's innate love for pretty
and bright surroundings. The chairs
were placed as if for delightful *tete-a-tetes*;
an upright piano stood near the east
window; a small tea-table, with its adorn-
ments of china and a silver tea urn, was
a silent witness to social chats; while
numerous pieces of *bric-a-brac* and dainty
scarfs, gracefully draped, gave a final
touch of color and refinement to the room.
Small wonder that its occupant wished to
remain within doors; but there could be
no choice in the matter. So with a half
sigh she crossed the room and entered
another, separated from the first by a
curtained arch. During the day-time
this adjoining apartment presented every
appearance of a well-regulated back

parlor. All that could be seen from the front room was a conventional centre table and a huge bookcase. The latter stood against the white, unpapered wall, its broad front boasting curtains of some thin, flowered material. At night these were pushed aside; and springs were revealed more dear to civilized humanity than even those from which flow the streams of knowledge. The fairy god-mother of modern invention went further, and transformed sundry chairs and tables into the additional belongings of "my lady's chamber."

Miss Walton occupied these two rooms in common with her friend, Martha Coggeshall, a Massachusetts girl, who was now a teacher in the "Number Two" building at the other side of the city, and who had set out for the scene of her labors at an early hour on this unpropitious morning.

Advancing reluctantly to a small table covered with feminine belongings, Elsa abstracted several pins from a cushion, with which she proceeded to shorten the blue serge skirt hanging in graceful folds to the floor.

This gown showed to advantage her rounded and symmetrical figure. It also suited well her blonde complexion.

"I shall wet my feet, I know;" she murmured dolefully, while making the circuit of the skirt. "There won't be half a dozen children out on such a day as this; and it is all nonsense for me to go down there. However, as I am subject, and not ruler, I may as well save my breath for the tug of war. Where's my umbrella?"

Shaking into place the shortened skirt, she glanced around in search of the needed article. Its tip was just visible below a curtain shutting off a right angled space on the opposite side of the room. Crossing over, she picked up the umbrella and laid it on a table; then removed her waterproof from its peg. While donning this indispensable wrap, she mused wickedly: "I just wish that I had some of those hideous garments advocated by certain leaders of reform. I'd put them on this morning. They would be much more suitable than petticoats for a tramp through this heavy rain."

But when once outside the door, a glorious sense of the youth and health that made possible for her a walk in this inclement weather chased away all rebellious feelings. The freshness of the damp air gave her new life. "I don't believe I want this umbrella;" she said, meditatively, with one hand still on the door-knob. "The rain cannot injure either mackintosh or sailor hat; and as for myself, I am neither sugar nor salt." Opening the door, she placed the umbrella inside.

Her spirits rising with the buoyancy of girlhood, Elsa ran down the steps. The rain-drops on her face were refreshing. She bent her neck backward to catch more of their coolness, only lowering her head when the gate was reached. It closd after her with a click. The water covering the side-walk proved shallow, and the crossing, a short distanc down the street, was safely reached. Here, the swelling pool was of greater depth; but by slowly and cautiously choosing her way, the opposite side of the street was gained with over-shoes still above high-water mark.

At this point the soft earth proved a snare indeed. With the first step into its treacherous depth an over-shoe was left behind. This had been carefully read-justed when she heard behind her the plash and thud of a horse's hoofs. The girl's face brightened. It might be some one coming whom she knew, and who would help her out of this awkward plight. The horse had slackened his pace, was abreast of her now, and she could see who was his driver. Delight-ful! it was Mr. Butler going to his ranch; and she had met him once or twice at social gatherings.

Miss Walton gave a bow of recognition. The man acknowledged the salutation by lifting his hat; and then—drove along.

The girl arched her eyebrows in astonishment. "To say the least, you are thoughtless," she ejaculated, looking after the retreating figure with an angry sparkle in her blue eyes. But there was no time to waste in idle exclamations.

With the next step forward, both over-shoes sank from sight in the black ooze. Dainty Elsa looked down in dismay at her wet and muddy gaiters, recovered the over-shoes, and, with these in one hand, made ready for a reckless plunge through the mud. But even now her headway was slow; for at each step, a small kid boot came up freighted with the sticky *adobe.*

Again wheels were heard near her; but this time she scorned to look up. The carriage was evidently coming toward "town." Just behind her, it wheeled; and almost before she became aware of its close proximity, a masculine voice said: "I will take you to school."

Miss Walton turned her head. Could it be possible that here was the very man who had so thoughtlessly driven past her. Would she ride now? No, indeed! The mischief was done. Both shoes were wet and muddy. And a little forethought on his part would have prevented this.

Seeing her hesitation, the man said: "I was so busy thinking when I passed you, that I neglected to ask you to ride. As soon as I came to my senses, I drove back."

He was now on the ground, one hand extended to assist her into the buggy.

The awkward apology and masculine assurance that she would ride only served to increase the ire of outraged youth and beauty. She was not the girl to stand meekly by the roadside, in a pouring rain, and wait for a man to complete his reveries before offering his needed services."

"I prefer to walk," she answered, with marked emphasis on the second word.

There are men and men. At this curt sentence, delivered with an air of *hauteur*, the greater number would have gone away at once; others would have repeated their offer of aid, and, after a second refusal, would have departed; while a still smaller number would have pressed their services upon her, and finanally would have left her, disgusted at her obstinacy.

Donald Butler was unlike any of these. The imperative mood was his usual form of expression, revealing the strong will power that commands obedience. He had no idea of going away and leaving a girl stuck in the mud, simply because, for some foolish reason, she had refused his assistance.

"I will take you to school," he repeated.

Unlucky construction.

Elsa looked longingly at the school building looming up ahead, and again said frigidly : " I prefer to walk."

" Yes," he assented pleasantly, " but this morning you are foolish to think of it. You should have taken a street car."

She would not tell him that, owing to a bad accident, the cars were off this morning, and she had no one to send for a public conveyance. It mattered not to her how foolish he might think her.

Still holding the muddy over-shoes in one hand, while her damp skirts were tightly clinched in the other, she attempted to go forward. But with the effort what a wave of humiliation swept over her! Each foot seemed weighted with pounds of lead. And there, in front of her, stood that insolent man.

He was tightening a strap at his horse's head. Elsa stole a look at him. She already knew that he was tall and well formed. His profile was good, very good; but his hands were large and covered with detestable freckles; and when he turned and accosted her again, she mentally concluded that the face was not a frank one. It could not be read at a glance.

"A woman has always the privilege of changing her mind," he remarked. "You had better do so now."

No reply.

Butler fell to studying Miss Walton. He coolly wondered how much of her fresh coloring was natural, and what proportion was due to the rain. After a critical survey, he decided that her beauty was of a rare order,—not his style though. He liked a brunette, and this girl was a blonde. Her present mood was also at variance with the sweet, infantile disposition usually accredited to girls of that type.

His horse becoming restive, he turned and laid a restraining hand on the bridle.

Metaphorically speaking, Miss Walton ground her teeth with rage. Why didn't the man get into his buggy and drive away? Oh, for that umbrella! With it she could at least hide her face from his insolent gaze. Thanks, however, to a strong constitution, she could stand here as long as he. But who would have thought of such an exasperating scene as this taking place? And it wouldn't have happened anywhere but in a little frontier city. The men here were so rude and uncultured!

O Elsa! and only two days before you had remarked to Martha that the gentlemen you had met in Phoenix were deserving of that epithet in a high sense.

"It must be nearly time for the ringing of the ten minutes' bell," she thought. As proof of this there came resounding upon the air its first peal. It increased the annoyance which she had been cultivating to genuine anxiety. She, the personification of punctuality, to be late to school! She wished she hadn't been so foolish in the first place. But now!

More imperatively sounded that warning bell.

A way of escape from her dilemma was suggested to her mind; it gained tangible form. It was possible to accept a seat in his carriage, and yet save her maidenly dignity.

Very condescending was the tone in which she addressed him: "Mr. Butler, owing to your importunings, you have delayed me, until I very much fear that I cannot reach my destination by the hour of nine. Tardiness is a shortcoming that I do not excuse in my pupils, therefore I must not appear late before them. I should have preferred walking, but now I shall feel greatly obliged if you will drive me to the school-building."

"It's a pity that you hadn't thought of this before;" was the laconic reply that set every nerve in Elsa tingling with anger. She drew herself up in haughty silence.

When set down before the school-building, she conveyed her thanks rather curtly, and then hurried within to the dressing room. Before the ringing of the last bell, there was hardly time to remove waterproof, change wet shoes for noiseless slippers, and otherwise make herself comfortable for the morning.

All through that session the query: "What manner of man is he?" would force itself into her mind with the teaching of numbers and reading.

———♦♦♦———

CHAPTER II.

"Those about her,
From her shall learn the perfect ways of honor."

WITH the advent of mid-summer came intense heat.   Not the gentlest zephyr was astir.   So still the calm that the very air seemed to be holding its breath in admiration of the varied crops and ripening fruits fast reaching perfection in this sun-kissed land.

To northern-bred Elsa the days were
often oppressive. One evening, after the
going down of the sun, she came out on
the veranda, hoping that it might be
cooler here than indoors. Within the
house, too, her thoughts reverted more
frequently to Martha who, in company
with other of Miss Walton's friends, was
out of the city. Thinking upon these
absent ones brought up pictures of
shady forests, flashing streams, and
winds, moisture laden. Elsa imagined
the delight of being with them in some
sylvan retreat or by the "cool sea-
waves."

The thought had in it no element of
discontent. Her critical and creative
powers weighed circumstances and always
found happiness in immediate environ-
ments. The air of Phoenix might be dry
and warm, but it was laden with spicy

odors of figs, grapes, peaches and other delicious fruits, while every table and bracket within doors held vases and bowls of fragrant roses. Furthermore, "the august three" had met the preceding night and decreed that she and Martha should be two of the few public school-teachers retained for the coming year. After standing for thirteen full weeks on the rickety fence of uncertainty, it was as good as a breeze from the sea-shore to be allowed to get down. Taking all things into consideration there was much to be thankful for.

In this comfortable frame of mind, she strolled down the path, and across the road and the vacant lot beyond, to the home of her friend, Mrs. Anson.

Before the house stretched a broad lawn divided by a wide gravel walk. Over this had been built an arbor, now covered with

luxuriant grape-vines from which hung
the ripened fruit. Her observant eyes
singling out an especially fine bunch of
the purple globes, Elsa possessed herself
of it and another that seemed equally as
good.

With these in her hand, she came to
the open door. The electric light at the
entrance of the porch was ablaze, illu-
minating, however, only the adjacent portion of the long central hall that served
as a family sitting room. Beyond was
shadow.

Elsa paused on the threshold. All
within was quiet. The electric fan on
the table at the rear of the room was in
motion; the breezes that it made stirred
the pink roses at her belt, and blew astray
the soft, damp locks on her fore-head.
The currents of air were so refreshing
that she remained standing motionless.

The graceful pose of the youthful figure, the happy expression of the flushed
face, and statuesque turn of the shapely
head made her a pleasing picture. At
least so thought the gentleman who, un-
seen, watched her from the lounging
chair placed where the shadows were
deepest.

After a short space of time, Elsa
knocked at the door. No one appearing
in answer to her rap, she turned to go
away. Donald Butler strode out into the
light. Elsa heard the step and faced
around.

"Why don't you scream?" was his
abrupt greeting.

"What for?" the girl asked wonder-
ingly.

"At sight of me."

Elsa gave an amused laugh. "I
didn't know that the appearance of an

ordinary man struck terror to a maiden's heart," she returned gaily.

The words "an ordinary man" were ambiguous, and the expression made Donald feel uncomfortable.

"But coming out of the shadows when you thought the room was vacant," he continued.

The man was in a mood for companionship, and had no idea of letting a pretty girl go, so long as he could hold her in conversation, especially one in whom his interest had been already aroused. Miss Walton had been in his thoughts many times since the adventure of that rainy day.

Elsa laughed again. "If your great grandfather had as suddenly appeared before my great grandmother she would, undoubtedly, have been much alarmed. We girls of today are braver, because we are wiser; we know that a dark place is quite likely to hold a man," she concluded archly.

Hardly were the words spoken when she felt sorry for their utterance.

Butler gladly took them up. "And the woman he sees within the light is the magnet that draws him from the darkness. It is a cause for congratulation, that you understand so well the mission of your sex."

"What you say is not true," cried this would-be opponent. "A man worthy of the name is prompted by his own self-respect to 'seek the light.'"

"But in nine cases out of ten, it is a woman's influence that draws him within that charmed circle," went on Butler. Here was not only a chance to air his pet theory, but to hear what this bright-looking girl might have to say on the subject.

Elsa moved away. "As your aunt, Mrs. Anson, is not at home, I think I must take my leave," was what she said.

The hat-rack was at the left of Butler. He reached out his hand and took down his sombrero.

"I have been intending to call on you, Miss Walton. I will walk home with you now," was the announcement made as they stepped out into the early, slumbrous night.

Elsa felt that the intention was of that moment's growth, and, for this reason, said nothing.

"Wouldn't you like to know that a man, for your sake, would always stand in the light; or, to do away with figurative language, always do what is right?" he persisted softly, when they were seated on the vine-wreathed piazza of Elsa's temporary home.

"I should have only contempt for the man who did right solely because *I* wished it," she answered; and there was a scorn and impatience in the voice that grated harshly on Butler's sensitive ear.

"*For your sake,*" were the magic words that in the bright future were to make Donald Butler give up all his petty vices, for instance, smoking. In the meantime, well! in the meantime, he was no worse nor better than other men. Just an average man. This thought has been very comforting to many a son of Adam.

As Elsa made no further remark, Butler observed, "Your remarks are quite Emersonian. They are self-illuminative."

"Why! are you a student of Emerson?"

Elsa exclaimed in surprise, quite ignoring the irony conveyed.

"I studied his works a little—while in college," returned Butler. Elsa thought that she detected the bitterness of disappointment in his voice.

It called to mind what his cousin, Myrldina Blake, had told her one evening some-time before; how Butler had been obliged to leave college because his father had failed in business, and soon there-after had sickened and died. Like many another ambitious youth, Butler might have worked his way through his remaining course; but there was another to be provided for. He declared that only in families where the men were sick, lazy, selfish, or lacking in mental ability, were the girls allowed to fight their own way in the world. His one sister should not go out as a bread winner; and so he had supported the two until she had married five years before. Then, with his few hundred dollars, Butler had come West and invested in ranch property that had since handsomely repaid him.

His chivalrous notion was wholly at variance with the advanced(?) ideas of the present day. Elsa knew this, and yet she honored the man for holding it. In theory it sounded very well to talk of a woman broadening her sphere by standing shoulder to shoulder with the sterner sex in life's battle; but Elsa, after careful observation, had failed to discover a single instance in which a woman had been actuated in taking this position by other motives than those of dire necessity; and in no case had this free contact with the world added one grace to womanliness.

Thus thinking, Elsa, herself, may have been a trifle old-fashioned; but it is said that the world is moving in a circle; and there are others, more enlightened than these two persons, who hold to the same opinion.

From these considerations, Elsa's heart grew strangely soft and she felt ready to forgive this man much.

He had become taciturn, and she exerted all her powers to entertain him; telling bright anecdotes, talking of the topics of the day, and relating bits of local gossip; all with a brilliancy and sparkle of word and manner that held enthralled the man sitting opposite.

"By the way, I received a call from Mr. Lord the other evening," she suddenly announced.

"He is a noble fellow, cordial and un-selfish," cried Butler with enthusiasm.

" I have proof of that," responded Elsa. "One day last winter Miss Coggeshall and myself went into the bank where he is employed, 'to soak a school warrant.'"

" To soak a school warrant!" exclaimed her caller.

"Yes, to soak a school warrant," repeated the girl, a charming gaiety in her voice and manner. "The expression may be slangy, but it is so commonly used here that one doesn't think of that."

" I wasn't thinking of its correctness but wondering what you could mean by it."

" As if you didn't know!" Elsa cried incredulously.

" I do not," he said with sincerity.

" Well then, Mr. Innocent, I will explain. At the end of each month, the school teachers are given what are termed 'warrants.' During the months of Sep-

tember, October, and November, there is
but very little money in the treasury.
Consequently, for the last two years, the
teachers have been unable to obtain their
wages until the latter part of December;
so, if one has no money and has needed
it badly, she has taken a warrant to a
bank, given it to the cashier as security,
and received for it something less than
its face value.   For this favor, she pays
the bank one and a half cents a month,
interest when she receives her school
money."

"That is outrageous," he cried as she
concluded.

"If you gentlemen think it outrageous,
then pay your taxes earlier instead of
loaning the money at usurious rates of
interest.   It is this that obliges us
teachers to go penniless or—'soak our
warrants.'"   Elsa   had   arisen   as   she

spoke and stood facing him with an air of girlish triumph.

The man's eyes kindled with a mystical fire, but the voice was quiet and composed that asked: " What did Mr. Lord have to do with your particular warrants?"

With a twinkle in her eye, Elsa established herself again in her chair and answered: " We told Mr. Lord that we wished to borrow money on our warrants. He took them: and as he passed us the amount asked for, he whispered, ' For goodness' sake, young ladies, don't ever tell any one that I was mean enough to ask you one and a half cents interest per month.' "

"You see," she added in explanation, "he had been here from the East only a few months and was not used to a westerner's way of doing business; or, I might say, until his arrival in this valley, he did not know what many easterners and westerners do with their superfluous cash. We girls had a good laugh when we got outside, but we shall always remember his kindness."

"When you need money again don't go to a bank for it, but come to me," he said in a whirl of feeling.

"Perhaps," coolly answered Elsa.

"I don't want a 'perhaps,' I want a promise," he insisted.

"If you have money to loan, I would as soon borrow of you as any one," was the reply given with much dignity.

His face fell. "You know that I did not mean it in that way," was the indignant exclamation.

"Mr. Butler, I could not use your money unless I did pay you interest."

"Then you are not willing that I should be your friend."

Elsa laughed softly, but with evident amusement. "O, Mr. Butler! I thought that you were a man of the world, and here you are talking like a school-boy. The moment I become your debtor, that moment rises a barrier between us. And as yet we are not even friends—only acquaintances."

Butler shifted uneasily his position. Having been courted and admired all his life, he did not like being held aloof in this practical, sensible way.

Through the open window, he caught sight of the low tea-table with its glittering array; and thinking, as most men do, that a pretty woman is never so charming as when brewing tea, he had a curiosity to see Elsa thus engaged.

The grapes that she had brought from Mrs. Anson's lay in a large leaf on the settee near him.

"Miss Walton," he exclaimed suddenly, "I could eat some of those grapes, if you would make me a cup of tea."

"*Tea*,"—this warm evening!" said Elsa with wide-open eyes.

"Yes," gaily returned Butler.

"It is too warm to sit within doors. Will you help me to move the table out here?" she asked, rising slowly from her chair. She expected that he would recall the expressed wish. He did not; and she passed into the parlor. Butler followed.

The table was brought to a convenient place near Elsa's chair, the alcohol lamp lighted, and before long the man held in his hand a cup of fragrant tea.

Elsa sat wholly within the light that came from the illuminated interior, while his chair was partly in the shadow. From this position, he could scrutinize closely every detail of her dress, every movement of her plump hands, and every expression of her winsome face.

Unconscious of it all, Elsa poured and passed him the refreshing beverage, met his wit with apt repartee, and otherwise played the perfect part of a well-bred hostess.

The time passed rapidly,—too rapidly, her caller thought. As he said "good evening," he lingered a moment with one foot on the lower step. Elsa stood on the veranda, looking down upon him. He opened his lips as if to speak, then turned abruptly, and in .a moment she heard the gate close behind him.

CHAPTER III.

"O, for a beaker full of the warm South!"

Where sunshine revels nearly all the
year, there must be much of merry-
making.   One autumnal day a long-
talked-of picnic excursion was made to
"The Hole in the Rock."   The eight
girls composing the party were up
betimes, and had met at the Tempe
road by seven o'clock.   All were well
mounted and good riders.   Four abreast,
they kept a steady, even lope; passing
the happy homes of ranchers set within
green fields of alfalfa; pausing awhile at
the Arizona Fall to admire the flashing,
foaming volume of water that plunges
down with rush and roar; looking with
beauty loving eyes upon the "Orange

Orchard" turned by the sun's rays into gardens of golden glow; and then cantering across the dreary desert with its tall cacti standing like grim sentinels. Presently, they ascended a little rise, bristling with mesquite and sage-brush, and the shadow of "The Rock" was reached.

After caring for the ponies and horses, some sought the broad, high arch that nature has hewn out of this stupendous crag; while the more adventuresome scaled the perpendicular rocks at the left; and from the dizzy summit, enjoyed a bird's-eye view of the country. When tired of this pastime, they descended to join the group that was making the cave-like opening at the south echo and re-echo with snatches of song and light or serious conversation, as best suited their varying moods.

It was here that Mrs. Anson found

them.   That they might come horse-
back, she had kindly consented to bring
the luncheons in her roomy carriage.
Shouts of welcome greeted her arrival;
for this tall, graceful woman, whose gray
eyes were luminous with good will and
happiness, was a universal favorite.
Many hands and merry hearts made
quick work of unpacking the inviting
collation. It was spread on a white cloth
under the purple awning of the over-
hanging crag.

At the conclusion of their feast, some
one suggested toasts, and Elsa Walton
was made mistress of ceremonies.   To
blue-eyed Bell was given "The Homes of
Phoenix."   The girl arose somewhat
reluctantly; but quickness of thought
soon dispelled all embarrassment, and
only a moment intervened before she
responded :

"At first it seemed surprising that my name should be called to answer to this toast; but on second thought I am sure it is eminently fitting. I came here only a few short months ago; and yet, I can truly say, that never for a moment have I felt as a stranger in a strange land. The doors of your hospitable homes are ever open to the sojourners who find their way here in search of health or pleasure. As one of them, I thank you for the many kindnesses shown these visitors.

Your home makers also deserve greatest praise for causing to disappear our ancient relative—the family skeleton. The house of *adobe* or wood has no narrow recess wherein can hide this unsightly form. Clothing can safely hang behind graceful drapery; but the family skeleton craves more seclusion.

Forced to live in light and air, he becomes clothed in flesh and blood; or, moping behind silken curtains, he weakens and crumbles into dust. Let us drink to the hope that the Southern Pacific railroad company may always, as now, charge such high rates for bringing lumber into Phoenix, that its inhabitants can never afford—closets."

A burst of applause followed this speech.

"I had no idea that the railroad was such a blessing in disguise," commented one.

"It is a bigger one than you think," quickly added another. "It keeps our merchants from failure. Their prices are exorbitant; but each George Washington of them declares that this is due to the high freight charges. Were this not so, these generous creatures would

sell their goods so low that before long
they would have 'to shut up shop.' The
Southern Pacific acts as a sort of balance
wheel, thus preventing such an awful
catastrophe."

Elsa now announced "The Coming
Sanitarium," to which Mrs. Anson replied
in chosen and well fitting words.

Following this, was given "The Sons
of Phoenix."

"I beg your pardon, Miss Toastmistress," quickly interposed mischievous
Edith, "but wouldn't it be more fun to
fill a cup to "The Bachelors of Phoenix?"

"It would do equally as well," replied
Elsa, whose merry smile answered the
sparkle in Edith's dancing eye. "Who
shall respond to that toast?"

"Myrldina," promptly returned Edith.

"Catch *me* replying to *that*," was Myrldina's inelegant retort. "I hate them

too badly. If I had my way, they should every one be put on a reservation."

"And why?" inquired slender, attractive Esther Fairfax, whose dark, limpid eyes had made more than one man willing to risk the shoals and quicksands of married life.

Saucy, piquant Myrldina flashed her blue eyes around the bright group, tossed back her golden head with a little proud gesture, and sagely remarked, "I could tell a great deal if I chose."

"Myrldina! Myrldina!" reprovingly sounded her aunt's voice.

But this spoiled girl—whose father and mother were away on an ocean voyage, leaving their daughter in Mrs. Anson's care—was in a mutinous frame of mind and had no idea of heeding the warning.

Clasping her hands about her knees,

she spoke in a peculiarly low, vibrating voice, which was, perhaps, her greatest charm: "I think it is something you all ought to know. To begin at the beginning, some time last June I was alone at Aunt Margarette Anson's. Cousin Donald came in with Mr. Ewing and Mr. Lord. They didn't have any better manners than to smoke in my presence, and soon the room was so filled with the horrid fumes that they couldn't see me; at least I think they couldn't, because they began talking about girls and getting married, the same as if I wasn't there."

"Perhaps they thought you were too young to heed what they might say," suggested some one.

"Well!" exclaimed Myrldina, "if I'm too young to be of any consequence, I'm not too young to talk." Then returning

to her subject: "You would have thought
from what they said, that all the girls of
the whole United States were sitting in a
row and meekly waiting for those two
older men to take their pick—Mr. Lord
didn't have much to say. Mr. Ewing
said that he would be glad to marry if
he were sure of getting a girl who was
a good cook."

" Nothing wrong in that, Myrldina,"
pleasantly interposed Mrs. Anson. "You
know it is a demonstrated truth that
a man's heart is reached through his
stomach."

"More's the disgrace to them," growled
her niece.

Again she resumed the thread of her
discourse: "Donald remarked that he
wanted to marry a girl with a low voice
and one who could preside gracefully
over the table.

He said that if he must sit opposite
her, three times a day, for perhaps thirty
years, he wanted to be sure she under-
stood her business. And then, worst of
all, they agreed to call on the young
ladies of their acquaintance, get each
one of them to serve refreshments, and
then take a vote as to which one was
prettiest and who made the best cup of
tea.

Now if they do call, don't you give
them a single thing—eatable or drinka-
ble," was the admonition of this adviser
who had recently celebrated her sixteenth
birthday.

There were ominous gleams in the
eyes of some of her listeners, while the
faces of others showed that they were
inclined to treat the whole thing as a
huge joke.   .

As soon as Myrldina had done speaking, Elsa, to prevent any discussion on what had been said, turned to Clara Gray and requested that she reply to the toast suggested by Miss Edith.

Clara divined Elsa's intent and arose at once:

"That the city is infested with bachelors cannot be denied; but we need not give one thought as to what shall be done with them. Like the Indians, they might be put on reservations; but they are hardly worth the expense that would have to be incurred. Cupid is sure to invade the Salt River Valley, and before his shower of arrows, these *singular* creatures must make way for a higher order of beings. We will not drink to the bachelors of Phoenix, but to the husbands following their exodus."

Much · laughter followed this unexpected response.

" Will Martha answer to ' The Daughters of Phoenix?'" graciously asked their toastmistress.

" In justice to the bachelors, this toast should be to the old maids," said Grace Huyson.

" I agree with you," answered Elsa.

Martha raised her glass and answered:

"The subject given me is one of which we know nothing. The old maids of Phoenix are but a myth; for, if such had ever existed, this highly oxygenated air would have restored to them the bloom of sweet sixteen. Phoenix can never have old maids—only jewels shining with such brilliancy that they need not the setting of matrimony to enhance their lustre. But if fate decrees for them these bands, may they be of gold and not of brass."

" Eighteen carats fine," added one gay

voice as their glasses were set on the cloth.

"Oh, no!" exclaimed another, "that's too fine for wearing use; fourteen carats fine will do nicely."

To Esther Fairfax was given the concluding toast of "Love."

Could it be that she was wholly unconscious of the knowledge that this divine god was even then drawing near?

Mrs. Hamilton—Mrs. Anson's sister—had also been invited to accompany these girls on their excursion. A previous engagement had prevented. At the noon hour she remarked this to her husband, and then added that it would be pleasant to go out and spend the evening with them.

"Why don't you go, then?" mentioned her husband.

"I don't like to go alone," replied Mrs. Hamilton.

"If you will go horse-back, I think that Lord will go with you; said Mr. Hamilton. "I can let you know in about thirty minutes."

Thus saying, he put on his sombrero and returned to the bank, where he found his assistant cashier busily engaged in writing. Hamilton went directly to the cashier's desk and began counting the gold coin there. In a few minutes he stepped to the telephone and asked for connection with No. 13. (This happened many times daily, for No. 13 connected with his own private residence.) Lord paid no attention to the one-sided conversation, until his employer said in a voice that might have burst the transmitter: "At what hour do you wish Lord to escort you, *horse-back*, to 'The Hole in the Rock?'"

At this, Lord threw down his pen in consternation, and exclaimed: "Great guns! what are you up to now?"

"I was merely inquiring at what time my wife wished you to escort her to the picnic," replied Hamilton, with an air of injured innocence.

"Great guns!" again exclaimed Lord, "I can't ride a horse. I never tried to but once, and then the ugly beast threw me into the air and I landed in the irrigating canal. Tell her—tell her—" and this young man, fresh from an Eastern college, stalked rapidly around the room in a vain endeavor to frame a sentence refusing the request of Mrs. Hamilton, and yet one that should in no way wound the feelings of the lady who had been very kind to him.

"Great guns! great guns!" he repeated. "A pretty escort I shall make, when I can't even stay on one of the four-legged brutes."

" Halloo! what is all this about, and why that wild look in your eyes ?" said Donald Butler, who had come in just in time to hear Lord's last remark.

"Our mutual friend is going to escort Mrs. Hamilton to 'The Hole in the Rock;' he is wondering where he can find a steed worthy of his horsemanship," was Mr. Hamilton's explanation.

Butler took in the situation at once. He had just come from his Aunt Louise Hamilton's, and there had heard of the picnic. His small, deep-set eyes twinkled as he said : " It is a shame to waste so much sweetness on the desert air, and I propose that Ewing and I make an additional escort for Aunt Louise to that enchanted ground."

He found Ewing in his office. This man pleaded business, but Donald carried the day.

In spite of Lord's belief that it was flying in the face of Providence to ride horse-back, when carriages were available, the four climbed the rise just as one original girl had propounded a puzzling riddle.

Mrs. Anson felt a little uneasiness on seeing who were among the late arrivals; but she soon found there was no cause for fear. If these young ladies had felt disposed to treat Mr. Ewing and Mr. Butler with other than cordiality, their good breeding would have over-ruled the impulse to resent a fancied insult.

" How nice that you changed your mind and decided to join us—even at this

hour," said Esther Fairfax, extend-
i   hand to Mrs. Hamilton.

"And are not the rest of us welcome? "
cried Ewing, looking steadily into the
dark orbs that had proved maelstroms to
numerous masculine hearts.

" Indeed, you are all most welcome,"
replied Esther, quickly turning aside
from his earnest gaze.

The remnants of the luncheon packed
away, they separated into groups of three
and four; some going in search of suitable cacti with which to make napkin
rings, and others again seeking the semi-
circular opening where a cooling breeze
is always circulating.

Elsa wandered away by herself. After
a little she sat down in a niche of the
rocky wall, and looked away to the
mountains glowing with their ever-chang-
ing hues caught from the luminous air.

But now she saw no beauty in them. Her thoughts were upon that July evening, and the idle talk repeated to-day by Myrldina. The girl was vexed with herself for her polite treatment of Mr. Butler at that time. "And yet," she mused, "I could do no differently. He was my guest, and so I was bound by all the laws of hospitality to make the hour pleasant for him."

There were approaching footsteps. Elsa heard the sound and turned her head to see the object of her meditations drawing near.

Donald Butler had come to " The Hole in the Rock " for the express purpose of seeing and talking with Elsa Walton. He had never repeated the call of that mid-summer evening. Elsa was without money and without influence. The future Mrs. Butler must have both. But

this peerless girl ought to marry, and
there were men in the city who, in place
of logical bumps, possessed those old-
fashioned organs called hearts.   He
would not stand in their way; but there
could come no harm from paying her
court — so long as the public did not
become cognizant of the fact.   This picnic provided a way of meeting her —
apparently without premeditation.

Coming near, Butler removed his broad
hat and leaned carelessly against the
gray stone.   He felt at a loss for words.

It was Elsa who broke the quiet.   "I
wonder why that mountain yonder is
called Superstition?" she asked, pointing
with one white finger toward the highest
peak, whose crest was transfigured with
a rosy radiance caught from the broad
streams of light.

"Beyond that mountain is the home of

the Apaches," replied Butler. "Owing to some rite of their religion, they dare not cross that mountain and descend into this valley; and for this reason, the Salt River Valley has never been invaded by that warlike tribe."

This bit of conversation was followed by an awkward pause.

Butler threw himself down on the ground where he could furtively watch. her face. It looked perplexed and troubled. There was also a coldness about the girl that illy accorded with the womanly side of her character revealed at their last meeting.

"I go into California to-morrow," he broke out. "I shall be gone three or four months."

·"Shall you?" politely responded Elsa.

Her indifference nettled him. He resolved to make a bold move. "I will write to you. You will answer my letter?"

"I never write to any of my gentleman acquaintances," replied Miss Walton, rising to her feet.

Butler was stung to the quick. There came over him a strong desire to break down the barrier of chilly reserve between himself and this girl. "Why will you persist in calling me a mere acquaintance? I would like to be your friend," he pleaded.

The careless remarks repeated by Myrldina were still uppermost in Elsa's mind; she felt half ashamed that these should influence her, yet she made no effort to conquer the weakness.

This was evident in her reply. "A girl who goes alone into a strange city should use caution. How do I know that you are worthy of a girl's friendship?"

The desirable parti and lineal descendant of a departed president caught his breath. The audacity of the girl! Springing to her side, he rejoined haughtily : "My appearance and my standing in the community are, I think, sufficient proof of my worth."

"Those go to make up a reputation," she assented. "But what chance have I had to learn anything of your character?"

"You have had the same opportunities to study me that I have had to know you," he said as crossly as a sense of his manhood would allow.

"But I have not yet asked for your friendship," she replied more gently.

True, she had not.

Without another word, Donald helped her over the rough ground to where a trio of girls were shooting arrows at a mark. Here he left her.

About sunset, the excursionists started homeward.

Mr. Ewing joined Miss Fairfax. He pointed out a bit of rugged scenery; then, dismounting, plucked a small flower and eulogized upon its beauty.

The voices of the party became lost in the distance. This had been his plan.

Alone with Esther—what joy!

Again he mounted, and their horses paced slowly side by side. A restraining hand grasped Esther's bridle rein.

"Do you know why I came out here this evening?" asked Levi Ewing, gazing earnestly into her face.

"Why! you came because the others did," stammered Esther.

"I came because I learned that *you* were here," replied her cavalier. "I love you. Cannot you care for me?"

For an instant her heart leapt with

happiness,—then sank. Trust her future
to a man who could speak lightly of
women? No!

She turned her eyes away to the crimson glow of the western sky.

The impatient lover could wait no
longer. "Cannot you be—*my wife?*" he
urged.

"I do not love you," was said so low
that only a lover could have caught the
words.

"But do you care for anyone else?" he
demanded.

To utter a denial would be making too
great a concession, so Esther remained
silent.

Levi Ewing let fall her horse's rein.
Over his face fell a shadow of pain, but
no word escaped him.

Esther started her horse into a lope,
Ewing did likewise, and in a few minutes

they came up with the body of the party.

So idle words, lightly repeated, separated these two hearts cherishing in reality a mutual affection.

> "O idle words!
> Your flight is ever on
> In heaven darkening the sun.
> By weary journeyings without delay,
> Ye wend your dreary way
> Unto the judgment day.
> Ill-omened birds!"

CHAPTER IV.

> *"And though he trip and fall,*
> *He shall not blind his soul with clay."*

IT was not until January that Donald Butler returned from his trip. The evening following his arrival, he stretched himself upon a couch in his aunt Margarette's sitting-room and prepared to enjoy himself in a domestic way. Myrldina was curled up in a big chair before the cheery wood fire. The third figure in this pleasing picture was their aunt, Mrs. Bowman, who had lately arrived from the East. Her head was bent low over a handsome bureau scarf into which she was putting the last stitches.

After a time, assuming an upright posture, she glanced severely at the full-length figure of her nephew, and exclaimed: "Donald Butler, I should like to know if you are never going to marry! Here am I sitting up nights and ruining my eyes that your rooms at the ranch may be presentable; you should have a wife to attend to these things."

"Aunt Henrietta Josephine, if you really think I need such an incumbrance, why don't you pick out one for me?" asked her nephew with an air of great humility.

"You would not marry her if I did," responded that lady with energy.

Donald chuckled. "I'm too deep for any of you women folks," he said gaily.

"I've known the depth of some people to take them straight down to the infernal regions," rejoined his aunt so quickly and earnestly that Donald winced.

His Aunt Henrietta Josephine's sharp remarks always made him uncomfortable,—to-night, doubly so.

"O, well! I mean to marry when I find a girl just suited to my mind," he said in a mollifying tone.

With blue eyes looking dreamily into the crackling fire, Myrldina began singing:—

> "Bachelors! bachelors!
> We find them everywhere,
> On the ranches, in the town,
> Looking here and looking there,
> For a dainty maiden, fair.

Each would have a pretty wife,
Whom he'd love as his own life,
But to choose aright takes time,
Later, marriage bells shall chime.
It is best to wait awhile,
Weigh each word, each sunny smile,—
Presto, change! the bird has flown,
And he has to live alone,
For a *younger, brighter* man
Improves his chances while he can.
And this is why the bachelors of P.
Companions are to 'The Old Maids of Lee.'"

Donald sat erect. "Myrldina Blake," he said with a frown, "that propensity of yours for making doggerel is getting to be a regular nuisance, and, for a girl of your age, it is exceedingly unbecoming." Thus having freed his mind, Donald settled back again to his former position.

Myrldina neither moved nor replied. Pitching her voice in a still higher key, she continued :

"And they're like them, you can see,
For they're *cross* as *cross* can be."

Whether her efforts at composition were productions of the moment, or made up in the seclusion of her chamber and then brought out as occasion demanded, no one knew; but they were always forthcoming, and Donald was most often the victim.

Their aunt laughing heartily, Donald reddened to his temples, and drawing a piece of money from his pocket, held it towards Myrldina, saying : " Here, I'll give you two bits for committing these lines to memory :

'Swans sing before they die; 'twere no bad thing
Did certain persons die before they sing.' "

" Thanks for your offer," unperturbedly returned the saucy girl, "but I prefer to make my own selections."

Mrs. Bowman glanced at the clock on the mantel. "It is nearing time for Margarette's invited guests to put in an appearance," she said, "and I think that this war of words had better cease."

Hardly had she done speaking, when the door-bell rang.

Myrldina assumed a more lady-like attitude, Mrs. Bowman ·laid aside her work, and Donald advanced to the door. It was thrown open, and the four persons standing without were invited to enter. The quartette consisted of Major and Mrs. Leadbetter, young Mr. Lord and Elsa Walton.

Donald had wondered if Miss Walton would come. He knew that in all probability she was aware of his return ; and also that he would be quite likely to make one of this informal dinner party, given in honor of Mr. Lord, who was about to depart for Dakota.

The thought of staying away, or of avoiding Butler, had not occurred to

Elsa; she frankly held out her hand to him, and was as ready with smile and word as if they had parted the best of friends.

To Butler this indifference was a hundred times more humiliating than any amount of stinging sarcasm or freezing silence could have been. He had full knowledge of the personal magnetism and worldly success that made him a power, and gloried in them. For his life, he could not see what prevented him from making an impression on this girl.

Mrs. Anson came in presently, and received her guests with her usual cordiality.

Later, there were more arrivals. Mr. Parkhurst, and Miss Coggeshall with Mr. and Mrs Hamilton.

After the dinner, this merry company

encircled the sitting-room fire for social converse.

Butler was at his best. He was seated on a couch near Martha's chair, and describing, in his own peculiar, racy style, pleasing little incidents of his trip.

"Well, Colonel!" cried their gentlemanly host to Mr. Parkhurst, who lived in the country, "are the roads dusty now?"

"They are fine," replied the gentleman addressed.

"Colonel," repeated young Lord, throwing back his fine head with a laugh, "I wish that some one would inform me as to the source of these masculine titles. Nearly every man one meets in the Southwest has one or more of these prefixes."

"Easiest thing in the world to explain," cried Donald, his face alight with ready fun. "This country, as you know, has rich mines, fertile valleys, and awe-inspiring scenery. Well! after all these had been placed within its borders, there yet remained a large area devoid of matter. In a fit of reckless extravagance, Nature made good the vacuity with titles of every known kind and degree; and to every man, who enters this enchanted land, she presents one of these marks of esteem and declares that he shall wear it—willy-nilly."

"But where is mine?" asked Lord.

"Oh! you lack that mark distinguishing the man from the boy—a mustache," answered his informer.

"But what about feminine titles?" piped Myrldina.

Oh!" wickedly returned her cousin, "Mother Nature knew that the title of 'Mrs.' pleases women best."

Mrs. Bowman's majestic figure rose to its full height. She had no idea of leaving her nephew triumphant in the field of wit. "And as Nature's favorite child, *man*, begged for the privilege of conferring this honorary degree upon the gentler sex, she kindly left it in his hands. Let us hope, young man, that you understand the great responsibility you have assumed, and that, before long, you will have sense enough to place that title where it belongs. You deserve to be fined for withholding it so long from its proper owner." This last was said with a mock severity that sent her hearers into convulsions of laughter.

"Never mind if the men have held a corner on that title for so long a time," merrily subjoined Mrs. Hamilton. "I should not be surprised if this inventive age broke the combine."

"If anything of the kind is attempted, there will be war to the knife," returned Donald, who involuntarily looked over to Elsa.

Before his keen glance, her eyes became veiled by their silken lashes. It filled Butler with a strange, sweet sense of exultation; for, insignificant as had been the act, it gave proof to the man that she had been forced to acknowledge the strength of his individuality. That this was only for a brief space of time did not lessen his triumph.

There was another beside Donald who had seen the girl's eyelids droop. Mrs. Leadbetter raised her eye-glass and glared suspiciously upon Elsa.

Never had she looked fairer,—a picture of blooming youth arrayed in white dotted silk cut away at the throat in a modest square and outlined with a soft, rich lace. Her immense sleeves of latest fashion came only to the elbow, and were finished with frills of the same fine lace.

Mrs. Leadbetter's eye-glasses dropped into her lap. Judging from the expression of her face, the vision of loveliness she had been contemplating was anything but pleasing.

Donald again concentrated his gaze upon the girl. His look was returned frankly and calmly.

With a half-sigh of defeat, he turned away and assiduously devoted his attentions to Mrs. Leadbetter. That lady's good humor was soon restored.

The little clock upon the mantel chimed out the hour of ten. At its sound the company rose and donned outside wraps, for all were to accompany Lord to the railroad station.

Under cheerful word and banter, the

men concealed their regret at parting
with a general favorite, while the women
cautioned him against the sudden changes
of weather which he would meet in his
journey.

When they had reached the depot, and
it was nearing time for the train to leave,
with eyes full of tears, impulsive Myrldina held up her pretty face; and what
could Lord do but imprint a kiss on the
willing lips?

And as history is valueless, if not correctly recorded, it must be confessed that
each feminine mouth was raised as its
owner gave her hand in parting. And
the gallant youth accepted graciously
this tribute of their friendship.

Oh, the courage of Young America!
What people can conquer a nation whose
young men possess such nerve as this?

When Mrs. Anson's guests returned

to her home, Elsa did not enter the
house. The brilliancy of the stars and
the freshness of the air appealed so
strongly to her that she sought the
hammock swinging in a corner of the
veranda. Into this she sank, and gave
herself up to a moment of quiet enjoy-
ment before joining the group within.

Suddenly a window was raised at her
left; and, from the rustling of the garments, she knew that a woman had sat
down in the low window-seat; then there
came a firm, masculine tread that halted
near by.

"Here I am, Mrs. Leadbetter, at your
disposal," said a voice that Elsa instantly
recognized as belonging to Donald Butler. "What do you wish of me?"

"Only to give you a little advice," was
answered in Mrs. Leadbetter's well-known
tones. "Come now! confess. I saw you

looking at Elsa Walton to-night in a way
that told your experienced friend that
you were on the verge of falling in love."

"And what of it?" was asked somewhat
coldly; for Donald Butler discussed his
affairs with no one. He would not even
take the trouble to tell this interested one
how entirely wrong were her surmises.

"You must not get angry," said Mrs.
Leadbetter in a voice meant to be con-
ciliating. "I only wanted to warn you
in time of her extravagance. Have you
noticed the expensive dress she has on
this evening?"

"I noticed only that it is becoming to
the wearer," replied the man who, while
he might speak slightingly of women in
the abstract, never encouraged the slan-
dering of one in the concrete.

At this instant, a shape flitted by the
window.

Mrs. Leadbetter's position was such that she did not see it; but Donald, standing with folded arms before her, caught sight of the white dress and golden hair.

Like a thunder-bolt from the clear sky had come the woman's accusation to the girl's ears. In her surprise, she had sat quiet—never dreaming of eaves-dropping. Aroused to a sense of her false position, she had hastily sought the room where a hum of voices told of more gayety.

It was not long before the guests went to their respective homes. Lord's departure had cast a damper over their spirits which could not at once be laid aside.

After the retiring of the family, Donald lighted his cigar, drew an easy chair before the glowing embers, and, from its depth, gave himself up to uninterrupted thought. Reluctantly, he admitted to himself that his thoughts were under-going a change. Miss Walton's illumin-ative remarks,—as he had been pleased to style her conversation of that July evening—had given rise to a train of thought to which the incidents of to-night had added more material.

The embers were fast dying out. Two-thirds of his cigar had been consumed; with a quick motion the remainder was sent flying into the grate. Then two long strides took him to the oak table whereon was standing a box of Havanas —his latest purchase; this, with its con-tents, followed the solitary weed.

As the pungent odor ascended into the air, Donald exclaimed aloud and half-deprecatingly, "My self-respect alone advises that. It isn't for the sake of any girl—ideal or in the flesh." Then he added, dropping his head shamefacedly, "Donald Butler, it is strange that you should live to this age before finding out that mind has height and breadth as well as depth."

———◆◆◆———

CHAPTER V.

" The secret of success is constancy to purpose."

An April day! vaulted sky so softly blue that no misty wreaths of fleecy loveliness were needed to enhance its beauty; purple mountains crowned with resplendent jewels by the lavish sun-god; onstretching fields of glossy alfalfa, in the midst of which waded, knee-deep, herds of sweet-breathed kine and steeds of noble pedigree; and, in the foreground, gold-flecked waters flowing through broad canals with rippling music.

Ordinarily, Elsa's soul would have been filled with the enchanting picture spread before her; but this matchless morning she sat by her window with that far-away look which tells of a mind too much preoccupied to take note of outward things, however attractive.

Martha had just left her, after bringing the ill-tidings that Mrs. Leadbetter's four children were sick with scarlet fever. It was this news that had shadowed the bright, young face, given a firmer expression to the delicately curved mouth, and made fainter the pink of the rounded cheeks.

Her thoughts ran somewhat in this wise: "It was not only ill-bred of Mrs. Leadbetter to pronounce me extravagant but it was downright cruel. More than that, it was a deliberate falsehood. That gown, with its expensive lace, was given

me by my god-mother when I graduated
from Normal College. Mrs. Leadbetter
knew this, for I had told her; and again,
she had always professed a great friendship for me, and I had believed in her.
As for Donald Butler, she has sung his
praises to me in season and out of season.
If she, herself, is so fond of him, it seems
a pity that she couldn't know how tan-
gled is the web of our acquaintance.
Love! forsooth," and here her lip curled
scornfully, "I know of none whose
acquaintance is less likely to end in marriage. Yet how gallantly he defended
me, or rather, struck aside her arrow of
malice! And not once has he referred to
that little adventure in the rain when I
was so silly; with all his faults, he can
be generous.

"But rambling on in this manner isn't
coming to the point. Shall I, or shall I

not, go to Mrs. Leadbetter and offer my services as nurse? As she doesn't know that I over-heard her remark, I think that she will accept me.

"There are three practical, common-sense reasons why I should do this thing. In the first place, it will give me a chance to put in practice what I learned in the hospital when I used to go there so much with dear Mamma; she often told me that sometime my knowledge of nursing might benefit some one."

The tears were now coursing down Elsa's cheeks; for thinking thus had brought vividly to her mind the fact of her orphanage. Her father had been captain of the "Isabel Rumball," and his wife had perished with him when that ill-fated vessel went down in the gale of 188— that wrecked so many noble ships sailing from the Atlantic Coast. This

had happened during Elsa's junior year
in college. Since then, her real home
had been with a relative in Philadelphia.
Wiping away the tears, she turned her
eyes again to the distant scene and continued her matter-of-fact soliloquy: "This
year there have been only seven months
of school.   At seventy dollars per month,
there is a sum total of four hundred and
ninety dollars; deducting board and
laundry hire, at thirty-two dollars per
month, there is left to my credit the sum
of two hundred and sixty-six dollars.
There are five months of vacation, and
my expenses cannot possibly be reduced
below twenty-five dollars per month—let
me figure never so closely.   One hundred
and forty-one dollars left; with such a
margin for clothing, books, and inciden-
tals, it is not at all strange that Mrs.
Leadbetter should set me down as being

extravagant." And the girl smiled ironi-
cally. "I need the money that she would
pay her nurse."

The next thought softened the severity
of her expression and brought a new,
eager light to her eyes: "And those
dear, little children! I do love every one
of them. I feel sure that I can relieve
their sufferings, and it may be that I
may even help to save their lives."

"But," said Reason to her, "you have
never had this disease, and it is very con-
tagious." Here her cheek paled, but fear
did not change the resolve forming in
Elsa's mind. "I am young and healthy,
and I hardly think there can be danger
for myself; yet if it should come, I could
die in no nobler service." Without further hesitation, Miss Walton went to
offer herself to Mrs. Leadbetter as nurse

during the children's illness. She was
received with open arms.

Of course her action became noised
abroad among their circle of friends.

The information was imparted to Donald Butler on a Sunday when he had
come up from the ranch. He was reclining in the hammock where Elsa had overheard Mrs. Leadbetter's uncomplimentary remark regarding herself. The restful stillness of the Sabbath had brought
a strange, sweet calm to the man's mind.
With dreamy eyes, he lay watching the
half-formed, graceful patterns of vine and
leaf with which the slanting evening sun
was chequering the veranda floor. Myrldina came rushing through the open
door, danced along the polished boards
and flounced down in a garden chair
before him.

Then she abruptly exclaimed : "Don-ald MacDonald Butler! it is of no use for you to lie there and revolve in your mind :—

> Which shall I marry? which, oh, which?
> Elsa is pretty, Lue is rich ;
> They both love me, they both make bread,
> Which, oh, which one, shall I wed?

Lue has already promised her heart, hand, and purse to young James Simp-son; while the fair Elsa has turned sister of mercy, and gone down to help Mrs. Leadbetter nurse her four children through the scarlet fever. I think it is a wicked shame; and, ten chances to one Elsa, herself, will have the awful disease, and be left dumb, deaf, or minus other of her senses." Here she paused simply for want of breath to go on.

Donald responded with heightened color, "I excuse that propensity of yours for making doggerel. I feel sure that you cannot help it. It is due to some spell laid upon you by the mermaids of the Southern Atlantic. A girl born on the sea and given the outlandish name of the ship on which her eyes first saw day-light is bound to be foolish sometimes."

It was now Myrldina's turn to redden, for this allusion to her name was always displeasing. Donald knew it, hence his shot.

But there was only good humor expressed in his cousin's retort: "You are wrong, my dear Donald. My doggerel, as you are pleased to name my poetic effusions, doesn't show foolishness but wisdom. It is an indication of second sight; and, as it enables me to get an inner view of the character of the Great Mogul of the Universe, I value it highly."

There were times when Donald felt a strong inclination to take hold of the saucy girl and shake her. This was one of them. There was truth enough in her rhyming hit deeply to wound his self-love. Wishing, however, for more information, he concealed his displeasure beneath his habitual dignified manner. It was well to proceed cautiously; for, if Myrldina discovered that he was questioning her with any intent, she would become as close-mouthed as the proverbial oyster.

"What do you care if Miss Walton has gone to help nurse Mrs. Leadbetter's children?" he asked with a show of indifference. "And even if she should sicken and die, what would that be to you?"

"Brute and monster!" exclaimed the now irate girl, rising and stamping her foot. " Isn't she the loveliest girl in the world, and didn't her father sail from the same port as my papa? "

"Don't fly into such a passion," quietly returned the man putting forth one hand and grasping the white wrist nearest him. Myrldina tried to wrest it away, but in vain.

"Sit down," he commanded, and she meekly complied.

Donald saw his opportunity and determined to follow it up. "What makes you so fond of this Miss Walton?" he asked.

"I was first attracted to her because her papa was a sea-captain—the same as mine is. Afterwards, I loved her for herself. She has been very kind to me." This was uttered in tones meek enough to suit the most domineering of men, and Donald was not one of these.

"She seems to me an ordinary girl," was his comment when Myrldina had done speaking.

Having very quickly recovered her spirits, Myrldina rose from the chair, moved back a pace, and quickly retorted: "Of course, to you and all your class, she is ordinary. If you superannuated bachelors had the eyes that Sam Weller said he *didn't* have, you couldn't tell the difference between a wax figure and a woman. For why? Your vision is obscured by your own self-conceit."

While she had been so pertly speaking, Myrldina had been backing away from him; and with the last word, she was away down the walk and hastening in the direction of Grove Street.

Donald had half a mind to call her back, but desisted. The mere knowledge that Miss Walton had gone to Mrs.

Leadbetter's aid was sufficient food for thought.

"What had induced her to do such a thing? It couldn't be friendship alone that had prompted her? At least he didn't think it possible. After all, it might be that she regarded him with such indifference that it mattered not how she might be maligned to him. Yet the fact remained that Mrs. Leadbetter had proved herself a Judas—and Miss Walton knew it. The girl must be an angel. Yet as she had her own living to earn, it was not wise for her to expose herself to such danger. Was there not some one who had authority to send her away? Perhaps if the Leadbetter family physician had full knowledge of the circumstances, he would forbid her staying longer." These were some of the thoughts that ran through Donald's

mind with lightning-like rapidity, the
while he reclined in the hammock, out-
wardly calm, but with an inward ebulli-
tion that threatened to engulf prudence.

After a time he bestirred himself,
sauntered down the walk, passed through
the gate, and wended his way to a certain
house on Pepper-tree Street. He found
the learned man of medicine in his office.
The latter failed to elicit anything very
satisfactory from this man who appeared
in the rôle of a patient. After a hasty
examination he was still further puzzled.
"Pulse normal, tongue clean, skin moist,
appetite good, digestion perfect. What
on earth could ail the man that none of
these should be deranged?" mentally
commented the baffled physician. He
scratched his head in despair. "Sleep
well nights?" he jerked out.

"Not very," boldly returned the other, with no qualms of conscience at thus stretching the truth.

"I see," joyously assented the M. D., "nervousness." And he straightway proceeded to weigh out some powders; one of these he dissolved in a small quantity of water and brought it to Mr. Butler.

Donald obediently swallowed the draught, settled back in his chair, and seemed in no hurry to pay his fee or go.

If the physician felt any surprise at these proceedings, he showed none; but patiently awaited the next move of his caller.

"Much sickness in the city now?" Donald asked.

"Not much," was the cautious reply.

"Any fever?"

"No, only two or three isolated cases of scarlet fever."

"I hear that Major Leadbetter's children have it."

"Yes," reluctantly admitted the physician.

"Whom have they for a nurse?"

The professional man broke through his customary reserve and exclaimed: "A Miss Walton. And she is fine, reliable in every way!"

"Ah, yes! I have met her once or twice," was said indifferently. "But isn't there danger of her taking the fever?"

"There is always a certain amount of danger," replied the other with dignity; "but with a certain amount of caution—

"But this girl is young," interrupted Butler, "and it cannot be that she fully understands the great risk she is running in helping to nurse those children."

The doctor was now gazing at him in mild-eyed astonishment. "I should say that she was twenty-two or three," he slowly replied; "and she certainly has the use of all her mental faculties."

Clearly there was nothing to be gained by this beating about the bush; and to Butler there was no other way of procedure. Half disgusted at himself for coming, and wholly angry at the obtuse physician, Butler paid his fee and took his departure.

Half-mechanically, he turned his steps to the street where stood Major Leadbetter's house. It was set well in from the highway, a hedge of handsome palms partially hiding from the passers-by the well kept grounds. Butler walked boldly in. Being a frequent caller here, he knew the rooms where the sick children lay. To the adjacent portion of the grounds he took his way, and slipped in among the over-hanging boughs of a knot of apricot trees. He did not analyze his motives in doing this thing. His thoughts becoming clearer, he determined on a plan of action. The newly risen moon was now sifting golden showers through the leaves. After the sick ones had been made comfortable for the night, it was quite probable that Miss Walton would come into the garden for quiet and fresh air. He would see her and try to dissuade her from the arduous and dangerous task she had voluntarily undertaken.

His surmises regarding her appearance were correct. Ere long she came quietly through a window-door and began pacing up and down the long veranda.

She was singing very softly a hymn. Butler could not distinguish the words;

but the measured cadence told him that it was something sacred. Either for fear of disturbing the childish sufferers or because the beauty of the night wooed her to the walks, she came in her light dress down the steps. Guiltily Butler moved farther back into the shadowing cluster of trees.

She was singing now in a fuller, clearer voice; and in the hush of the evening these words came plainly to the ear of the listening man:

> "'Lead thou my feet! I do not ask to see
> The distant scene; one step enough for me.'"

Instinctively, he raised his hat from his brow and stood with bowed head. Another line of the hymn, full of devout meaning, floated to him upon the sweet contralto voice:

> "'Pride ruled my will; remember not past years.'"

The singer gave the words no unusual

expression; but the man's heart was so attuned that it seemed to him as if she stood a saint at the throne of grace interceding for his soul.

"'Pride ruled my will:'" Butler felt the sentence a true confession of all that had filled his brain and heart and soul during his manhood.

"'Remember not past years:'" this time the words were wrung from the depths of a strong man's heart.

He would not try to turn the girl from her purpose; he felt that not only would his arguments be in vain, but sacrilege against the higher nature unconsciously revealed to him this evening.

He remained concealed until Elsa had returned to the house.

On his homeward way a sudden strong resolve took possession of him; but past events loomed up in the way of its accomplishment. The agony of doubt brought a cold sweat to his forehead. Then, with the courage born of high resolution, recalling the words: "One step enough for me," he said firmly to himself, "I know that step. Let it suffice — at present."

———✠———

CHAPTER VI.

"And, after all, what is a lie? 'Tis but the truth in masquerade."

In council sat the knight, the knave, the fool,
An' argered long an' late about the school.

In this land of Italian softness, each delightful day so quickly follows another that one must stop and think before naming the solar month—if he would do so correctly. July alone pauses with a solemnity that gives no chance for erring.

On one of the warmest of these warm evenings, the newly elected school board of Phoenix held its first meeting.

Mr. Morgan, the chairman, had returned to his office soon after dinner for the purpose of completing some unfinished business. This done, he took out his watch and found that it lacked but twenty minutes of half past seven—the hour of appointment. Sitting down in front of a desk, he opened a drawer and took out a bundle of letters. These he assorted in two heaps. The one at his right consisted of only fourteen; having counted those at the left, he gave a prolonged whistle.

"Whew!" he ejaculated, "eighty-four applications for fourteen positions." Thrusting his hands into his pockets, he stretched his long legs under the table and surveyed, with a dismayed

face, the innocent squares before him.
"And I'm to help elect the corps of
teachers for the ensuing year. What
are my qualifications? I'm sure that I
don't know; but my friends must, for
they said that my serving on the school
board would be of inestimable benefit to
the city. But it appears that this is true
only so far as I follow the advice of Tom,
Dick, or Harry, whose sisters, aunts, or
cousins are, according to their disinter-
ested judgment, the only ones capable of
properly instructing our specimens of
Young America. Thanks to my wife, I
do know a little something about Froebel
and the new education. This knowledge
may be of some use to me and it may
not. At any rate, I'm in for it now!"

Steps were heard slowly ascending the
stairs, and in a few minutes there entered
a feeble-looking man of about fifty years

of age. Dropping into the chair that
Mr. Morgan handed him, the new-comer
said in a hollow voice, "Goin' up stairs
winds me—winds me."

This man was slender, bowed, and nar-
row-shouldered; and notwithstanding the
excessive heat of the day, he wore a long
mouse-colored coat buttoned to his chin.

After a moment's pause, he said a little
hoarsely, "This is importint bisnis that
we have to do to-night—have to do
to-night. Have you seen the Lord about
it—seen the Lord about it?"

"Well, no!" answered the other somewhat brusquely, "I have been inter-
viewed by so many myself, that I have
had no time or chance to ask any one's
opinion."

"Trainin' the young is importint bisnis, mister, and we want to make a good
chice—a good chice. We want those who

are on the Lord's side—on the Lord's side."

There now appeared a brisk, energetic man of medium size. He would have been called good-looking had it not been for the deep scar over his left eye, which he had carried for many years. It was not an honorable blemish, but one gotten in a drunken broil in pioneer days. His small, steel-colored eyes were deep-set and roved restlessly about.

"Ah, good evening, Deacon! How is your cough?" he inquired of the stooping figure.

"About the same, Jedge, thank yer—thank yer," feebly replied the Deacon.

"It is evident, Morgan, that you are ready for business," the Judge then said, going to the table, carelessly picking up an envelope and hastily scanning its contents.

"Yes," was the reply, "and, as the Deacon says, this is important business, and the sooner we get to work the better."

"I reckon I'm ready," observed the Judge, throwing down the letter and seating himself in an office chair that stood on the opposite side of the table and in front of Mr. Morgan.

"I think," said that gentleman, "we should consider first the applications of those who have been teaching here for the past year."

"I reckon that I agree with you," pleasantly assented the Judge.

"Then we will take up the application of the city superintendent first. He wishes to be re-elected. What is your mind, gentlemen?"

"He's a leetle slow—a leetle slow," said the hollow voice.

"I reckon I know of a better man,"

remarked the Judge. "Mrs. Severns says that Mr. Pooldar is twice as good as the present one."

"I also have a name to propose for that position, gentlemen," said Mr. Morgan. "It is that of Mr. Storman of Dunboro' University. He has travelled abroad, has received the degree of A. M., and is at present principal of a Normal School in Ohio. Owing to the ill health of his wife, he wishes to come here to live; and, for this reason alone, wishes a position in our schools. He is highly spoken of by leading educators."

"What are his politics?" asked the Judge.

"I know nothing of his politics and don't care what they may be," impatiently replied Mr. Morgan. "The best man for the place is what I want."

The evening was very warm; and the

chairman of the school-board wished that
he were well out of this business. But
he thought of his three children; and,
realizing that the instruction and influence under which they would be placed
for the coming year rested in a measure
with him, he straightened back in his
chair and began again: "Gentlemen, who
is to be superintendent of our schools for
the coming year? I wish to see the salary raised and a more broadly educated
man than Mr. Andrews filling the chair."

"The city is payin' too much now—
too much now," croaked the economical
Deacon.

"I reckon that I'm in favor of increasing the salary," said the Judge, "and I
will vote to do so if Mr. Pooldar is elected;
otherwise, I will not."

"But," interposed Mr. Morgan, "his
qualifications are no better that those of

the present incumbent. So, why make the change?"

"Well! Mrs. Severns said that she thought this man would be twice as good as Mr. Andrews; and as he is not satisfying everybody, I thought it a good idea to make a change of some kind."

"That is an erroneous idea," said Mr. Morgan. "If you cannot better things, let well enough alone."

"I shan't vote for the pay to be riz— the pay to be riz," doggedly whispered the Deacon.

"I put the question again," said the chairman. "Who shall be the city superintendent for the coming school-year?"

"I reckon I cast my vote for Mr. Pooldar, and also for an increase of salary," said the Judge.

"I vote for Mr. Storman of Dunboro'

University, and an increase of salary,"
announced the chairman.

"I votes for neither—for neither,"
spoke the hollow voice. "I votes for
Mr. Andrews, and no raise in pay—no
raise in pay."

That Mr. Pooldar would be no improve-
ment over the present officer, Mr. Morgan
well knew; and, as the man he wished to
see elected met with no favor whatever,
he seconded the Deacon's vote. Under
the circumstances, this seemed best;
although he frowned deeply as he saw
the Judge record the name of Mr.
Andrews.

The chairman took up another application. It was that of an upper grade
teacher. "Miss Rosson wishes her position another year," he said. "As she has
done good work, I move that we retain
her."

At this point the Deacon picked up her letter of application which the chairman had just laid on the table.

" I votes agin her—agin her," he said excitedly.

"And why? " coolly asked Mr. Morgan.

" Jest look at that—look at that," he cried, at the same time pointing with a bony fore-finger to the page before him.

The chairman looked searchingly adown the lines; but, seeing nothing to cause this outbreak, he said, " Well! what is it? "

" T-h-e-r-e—t-h-e-r-e," spelled aloud the Deacon. "A girl who makes a blunder like that, hadn't ought to have a school— hadn't ought to have a school."

" That word is spelled correctly," answered Mr. Morgan, opening his eyes in astonishment.

" It ain't—it ain't," contradicted the

Deacon. "T-h-a-i-r—t-h-a-i-r, is the way to spell it. Ain't that so?" he inquired of the Judge.

The Judge smiled. That Miss Rosson was one of the best of teachers, he knew. But she was no favorite of his; for had not his wife called on her and she never returned the call? Besides, her masculine relatives differed from him in politics. Nothing to be gained by voting for her. A man received no pay for this work and he must turn it to some account. If daughters of men of his own party were given the position, he could count on certain votes at the next election; and he hoped to run for mayor. These were his inward thoughts, but aloud he said: "I reckon the spelling is all right, but there are other things to be considered. I reckon that it would be better to put Miss Stafford in her place."

"Why, Judge!" exclaimed Mr. Morgan, "she does not possess the qualifications of the girl you would evict."

"That may be," assented the Judge, "but I reckon that she knows enough to teach the pupils of that grade; and if she don't, why! lower the grade; and as her father lives here and pays his taxes here, I reckon that she ought to have the school, even if she is not as well educated as the other."

The chairman picked out a letter from the pile at his left, and proceeded to read it aloud :—

GENTLEMEN :—

I desire a position in your city schools. I am a graduate of Alhambra College, and of the Lakeside Normal in Michigan. For the past three years, I have been an assistant teacher in Hartford Academy, Illinois. For testimonials,

I refer you to G. S. Lane, principal of that institution, and to Prof. Dash of Arizona Territorial University. An early answer is desired.

Yours truly,

MARIA SNOW.

When he had finished reading the letter, Mr. Morgan said, "I should like to see that young lady put in Miss Rosson's place—if you feel that the latter must be evicted." The words were spoken deferentially, for Mr. Morgan's sole object was to work for the good of the city schools. Then he went on, "Miss Stafford has had no experience. The professor, to whom Miss Snow refers us, is a man of liberal education and sound judgment, and a testimonial from him in her favor should count for a great deal."

The Deacon gave him a combative look.

"Them perfessers are men who don't

think on nothin' but ketchin' bugs and mixin' messes in glass dishes—mixin' messes in glass dishes. I've been down to see their school, and so I knows—I knows."

Here Mr. Morgan's ire got the better of his judgment. Springing to his feet, he brought his clenched fist down on the table and roared, "Confound it! I'd like to know how in the name of common sense a party ever happened to put such as you on the school board. This comes of mixing up politics with school affairs."

The Deacon uneasily moved his chair; the Judge coolly smiled; while Mr. Morgan, instantly ashamed of his hasty temper, mopped his perspiring brow and sat down again. All the heat of the day seemed concentrated in that one room.

Now was the time for the Judge to

make a move. "I reckon that I cast my vote for Miss Stafford," he said.

The Deacon moved his chair further away from Mr. Morgan before he found courage to say, "I votes for Miss Stafford. I do—I do."

So the name of Miss Stafford was recorded below that of Mr. Andrews.

Several applications followed this; the writers being re-elected or evicted with equal want of just discrimination.

Then came to hand the letters from the primary teachers; among which, by the way, were those of Esther Fairfax and Martha Coggeshall.

The epistles being duly read, the chairman inquired what should be done with them.

"I reckon that I don't think much of the goings on of these Kindergarden teachers," said the Judge, bringing his

crossed leg to the floor and sitting around
squarely in his chair. "Mrs. Severns
says how as the first year they teach the
children to draw a cat, the second year to
rub it out, and the third year to spell
'cat.' I reckon that she knows. I reckon
that it will be a mighty sight better to
let those three kindergarden teachers go,
and hire girls who will work."

"I'm agreed with yer—agreed with
yer," whispered the Deacon. "My chil-
derns bring papers home from school, all
doubled up—all doubled up. Little bits
of squares, three-cornered ones, and
round ones—and round ones. And Mrs.
Severns says how as they play in mud
there—play in mud there. Roll it round
and round in their hands, and make what
they call 'sp'eres'—what they call
'sp'eres.'" And warming to his subject,
the Deacon put his two hands together,

and rubbed one upon the other with a slow circular motion, to demonstrate the making of " sp'eres."

Froebel, the new education, law of unity, and a dozen other things pertaining to Kindergarten work, became a confusion of ideas in the chairman's head; but not one principle could he advance to defend these progressive teachers. He could only say: "I know these teachers are hard-working and capable. Their instruction is of the best, and you must see that it is wise to retain them." The Judge and Deacon did not see this; so these instructors were evicted in a body.

Miss Walton's application came next.

" She's a mighty pretty girl and a right smart one," commented the Judge when her letter had been read.

"Mrs. Severns says how she is too flightin' — too flightin'," criticised the

Deacon. "She seed her ridin' two different times with two different men—two
different men."

Mr. Morgan's lip curled scornfully, but
he said quietly, "Her qualifications are
of the best, and I move that we retain
her."

"Well," slowly and somewhat reluctantly observed the Judge, "she's a right
bright girl, but holds her head too high
for this new country. We'd better try
somebody else."

The now thoroughly tired Deacon nod-
ded his head in the affirmative and feebly
whispered, "Too flightin'—too flightin'."

Mr. Morgan was helpless.

It was late, very late, when the last
teacher had been elected. After the
Judge and the Deacon had gone, Mr.
Morgan returned the letters to their
drawer, locked it and put the key in his

pocket. Then rising, he wiped the perspiration from his face, and set his chair in its customary place. This done, he put on his sombrero, passed through the door, and as he made it secure for the night, he muttered: "I hope that the meeting of this evening is not a fair sample of what usually takes place. But teachers certainly lack progression, when year after year goes by and they do nothing towards limiting the power of school boards; who, if they possess the requisite educational qualifications, too often lack a practical knowledge of methods. Pedagogical associations must have the life of Egyptian mummies."

CHAPTER VII.

" Truth is the highest thing that man may keep."

DONALD BUTLER'S ranch lay six miles
southeast of the city. Half of it was
given up to the cultivation of raisin
grapes; while the remaining portion was
sub-divided, the several divisions bearing
thrifty trees of apricot, peach, fig, olive,
and orange. Every part of this fruit
farm gave evidence of the owner's method-
ical mind. Even the irrigating canals
and ditches were so cleanly cut that
Dame Rumor slyly whispered they were
sand-papered by Butler's own hands.
This report, however, cannot be vouched
for, as the good woman mentioned has
passed her three score years and ten, and
so her memory is not always reliable.

The ranch house was a two-roomed adobe, encircled with the veranda so indispensable to a southern home of even the most modest pretensions. The same order and neatness shown outside was revealed within; but for the consolation of those masculine celibates whose rooms are *chaos*, let it be known that, about once in so often, the house-wife of a neighboring ranch was hired to sweep, dust and arrange these apartments. Butler flattered himself that the matter was kept a profound secret. In so level and open a country, though, secrets can not well hide, and this one was not the exception that proves the rule.

During the summer months, he was seldom absent for any length of time; as it was then that the picking and curing of figs and grapes demanded his personal supervision.

One evening, the work of the day concluded, he seated himself in the front
room with the design of reading the
latest fruit journal; but the page before
him proved not of sufficient interest to
hold his attention; every now and then
his glance would wander through the
open casement at his right and across the
trailing green of vines stretching as far
as his eye could reach.   To-night he
viewed the scene with a double satisfac-
tion, not only because it represented the
results of his labors and savings; but
because this day he had shipped the
largest consignment of fruit that had yet
left this ranch.   It was but natural that
he should think upon his success with a
certain amount of pride.

From contemplation of his profits, his
mind wandered into the future; and he
saw, in place of the humble adobe, a

stately edifice with broad avenues leading thereto. He even decided from which point of the compass should come the carriage drive.

His eyes following down a narrow path, he was surprised to see in the distance a moving cloud of dust that fore-told a coming horseman. Butler watched the drawing-near with interest; for, at this season, visitors rarely ventured through the drifts of dust that lay between the city and the ranches.

When, at length, he discerned a female figure sitting the horse, his amazement was increased; before long, the lope of the steed brought him to a halt before the office. Butler sprang from his chair, and reached the door just as Myrldina slipped to the ground.

"What has brought you here in this plight?" he exclaimed bluntly to the girl, while she was deftly fastening her horse by the bridle rein to one of the posts that served to support the veranda.

"Is any one at home sick or hurt?" he asked anxiously.

And truly it did seem as if nothing short of a severe illness, or a serious accident, could have caused Myrldina to ride through the dust and heat of this July day. The horse was covered thick with foam and dust; while his rider was completely enveloped in the multitudinous particles that filled the air almost to suffocation.

To her cousin's question, Myrldina shook her head in the negative.

"Then," Donald dryly suggested with a movement of the head toward his sleeping-room, "I think that you had better go inside, wash your face and hands and afterwards we will discuss whatever has brought you here."

She was now unfastening the cinch-strap. Her cousin came to her aid, saying, "I'll remove the saddle; go inside."

With a quick motion, not ungraceful, Myrldina gave her sateen skirt a shake that sent the unstable overdress flying on every side. Obedient to Donald's wish, she then passed into the inner room; emerging in a short space of time with hair newly smoothed, and face freshly bathed.

"Well?" he began encouragingly, placing her a chair before his own.

The girl needed no second invitation. "O Donald!" she broke out, "the new school board met last night and evicted many of the teachers — Miss Walton among the number. She— with others— has staid here—ever since April—expecting reappointment. Their eviction is just too mean for anything! Can't something be done about it?"

"And is that what brought you here?" he asked, almost scornfully.

Myrldina began to cry. "I—I—feel that I had something to do with their eviction; and I thought that perhaps *you* could do something towards making the school board put them back in again—especially Miss Walton."

"How could you possibly have anything to do with their eviction?" Donald asked in tones of wonderment.

Myrldina wiped her eyes, pocketed her handkerchief, and promptly proceeded to impart the desired information: "You see it happened in this way. Mrs. Severns,—the meddlesome old thing—

"And who might Mrs. Severns be?" interrupted her cousin.

"Why! that woman who lives not many blocks from Aunt Margarette's, in that house having six immense umbrella trees in the front yard. Now and then she teaches a term of private school; and as she has a little knowledge of the three Rs, she meddles in the affairs of the public schools every chance she can get."

Thinking this sufficient explanation, Myrldina continued: "I was going by there one day just as Mrs. Severns was coming out of a side door with a bowl of something hot in her hand. It being a warm day, and she a little lame, I offered to carry the dish for her. She thanked me and said that it would oblige her greatly if I would take the bowl to Deacon Smart. I did so; and as I go right by her home when I am out for a constitutional, I have carried the deacon many a bowl of hot soup during the past few weeks. Mrs. Severns was always at the gate ready to waylay me; and I didn't mind it in the least, for I thought that I was doing a good deed. But it must have been her hot messes that influenced the deacon to vote as she wished. He told Mr. Wight that he didn't vote for the re-election of these teachers simply because Mrs. Severns asked him not to. And to think that I should be the instrument to effect her plans! I *never, never* would have carried those dishes, if I had had the slightest idea that I had so many girls in—in the soup." And again Myrldina's face was hid in her handkerchief.

Having a keen sense of the ludicrous, this recital was too much for Donald. Lying back in his chair, he gave vent to peal after peal of laughter, which only ceased when Myrldina hastily rose, eyes flashing, and indignantly exclaimed : "I didn't ride down here to be laughed at! I came for your help!"

Donald sobered instantly. "Why, my dear child!" he said soothingly, "I can do nothing. I fail to see how anybody can do anything about it. The school board have not only decided whom they will retain, but they have, in all probability, published their decision in the city papers. Isn't it so?"

"Yes," sobbed Myrldina.

"They are supposed to represent the city," he explained, "and their decision must be accepted without question. Your friend, Miss Walton, will have to look elsewhere for a position," he added, after a minute's pause in which it seemed to him that his heart dropped in his breast like lead.

"But the injustice of it all!" cried Myrldina. "If they were all intelligent men it wouldn't seem so bad. But the Deacon is an old fool, and the Judge would sell his soul for two bits." And then she questioned, as had Mr. Morgan the previous evening, "Why are such men permitted to serve on school boards?"

To this Donald made no reply. He was standing with arms folded, lips tightly compressed, and eyes looking steadily before him.

Finally, he said almost sternly: "Now, Myrldina! you are wasting you strength in shedding these useless tears. You must learn to look at things in a more philosophic light. I fear that I can do nothing towards keeping your friend in the city; but"—and there came a long pause, followed by the completion of the sentence slowly and resolutely—"I will do what I can."

However she might tease him, Myrldina's faith in Donald was unbounded. It now revealed itself in ecstatic words: "O, you dear Donald! I know that you can make it all right. You always do."

Donald did not feel so sure of success, but he did not lessen the girl's ardor by saying so.

"What are you going to do?" she questioned cheerily.

"A diplomat doesn't tell his plans to any one," promptly returned Donald.

In no way disconcerted by his answer, the girl continued, "Well, *when* are you going to do it?"

Her cousin laughed. "You are a veritable woman, Myrldina. There is no crushing of your curiosity; but if it will please your ladyship to know, I'm going back with you. Before long the moon will be up."

The hot lustrous night was odorous with sweet perfume of tree and plant, when Donald and Myrldina rode back to the city. With the instincts of an artist, the girl drank in the beauties of the landscape, softened by the light to an inconceivable beauty.

The man was silent, too; but for far different reasons. Not for a single instant, since that evening in the Leadbetter garden, had he lost sight of the singleness of purpose that had triumphed over his baser nature. It came to him this night with a new meaning. He felt that he was nearing the crisis of his life. Let that hour bring him weal or woe, he would never swerve from this duty he owed himself.

A half hour later, he stood before a mirror in one of his Aunt Margarette's rooms making a careful toilet. This done, he paced twice the length of the floor before essaying courage to pass out. What flood tides must sweep over his soul before he would again enter this room!

Without meeting any one, he reached Mrs. Durgin's house. He gave a sigh of relief when he caught sight of Miss Walton sitting in the golden glow of light that flooded the veranda. She was reading the evening paper, and Butler saw that she was alone.

She greeted him with a few commonplace words and motioned him to a chair near her. Butler was surprised to find her so tranquil. He had pictured her with brow dejected and spirits drooping; but instead, she looked as fresh as the crimson bud fastened in her hair.

He had decided that he would not feign ignorance of her eviction by the school board; neither would he ignore the fact.

After a moment's chat on the weather, he asked, " Do you leave the city soon? "

" I intend going day after to-morrow," was the reply.

" The circumstances are inauspicious that hasten your departure."

" It was not wholly unexpected," she answered carelessly. " You know that in the West public school teachers dine with their grips by their chairs." By the way, this remark which her caller thought very bright, was not original with Miss Elsa. It was a quotation from a leading New York educational journal.

" You do not seem to feel badly at going," he continued. " I presume, though, that this is partly accounted for by the knowledge that all women of to-day are more or less cosmopolitan.".

" Who says so? " asked Elsa with simple directness.

" Why! we hear it at the club, read it in the papers, and have it hurled at us from the pulpit," answered Donald, provokingly twirling his mustache with the air of one who feels that he can prove all he asserts.

The color on her cheeks had deepened a little, and the light of her eyes betrayed more eagerness; beyond this there was nothing to indicate that the remark had aroused in her any spirit of opposition. Donald, however, noted the slight change and resolved that he would harass her further. Her cool self-possession and indifference held him at a disadvantage.

"Cosmopolitism doesn't add to a woman's attractiveness," he said. " Women make a mistake in seeking so many

avenues of employment; they are losing
their chief charm in so doing."

"Why do they seek these employ-
ments?" she inquired with some *hauteur.*

"An eminent divine" (Donald gave his
name) "has said it is because a woman
likes to prove that she is as good an
oarsman as a man."

"I have never known a woman to seek
out a prominent place for any purpose
but as a means of self-support," quietly
remarked Elsa, but with eyes flashing.

"But she could earn her living in a
less conspicuous way," suggested Donald. "There is no need of making such
a tumult about it."

"It seems to me that the club, the
press, and the pulpit are responsible for
this tumult you mention. The women
are busy about their work; and these
three powers—controlled almost wholly

by men—create the tumult." Insurrec-
tion was now visible in every lineament
of the flushed face.

"But they are losing their womanliness," argued Donald.

"I think your premise is wrong,"
soberly returned Elsa. "If a woman is
forced by circumstances to earn her
bread, it seems to me that it is no more
womanly to content herself with crumbs
than it is to secure a slice, or perhaps a
loaf for herself. For my own part, I
intend getting just all I can in an honest
way."

"Your remark carries conviction with
it," observed the man. "I own a ranch
and I should hate to be ousted from it;
but if you should get after it, I feel, in
the innermost recesses of my soul, that I
should have to turn it over into your
hands. I may as well yield it up now,

gracefully, and without further parley."

Elsa stood up and looked at him in round-eyed wonder.

Butler felt that now was the time to drop his bantering tone and speak more earnestly. "I came here this evening for a purpose," he said. "One year ago this month, some words carelessly spoken by yourself, deeply impressed me;—so deeply, that they changed the whole tenor of my mind regarding certain things. Until then, I had been wholly absorbed in making a success of life from a worldly point of view. When it occurred to me—as it sometimes did— that my sordid nature could not reach out in charity towards my fellow-men, nor rise to meet the 'Source of all Truth,' I would silence conscience with the thought that in the dim future there should come, into my heart and home, a white-souled woman whose influence should make of me a better man. Your casual remark showed me that her love could not be based on respect;—therefore it must always remain cold."

From this he went on to speak of Mrs. Leadbetter's perfidy, Elsa's forgiveness, and the scene in the garden to which he had been a witness.

"My regard for you has kept on increasing," continued the mellow, alluring voice, "until you are the one woman in the world for me. I love you deeply— truly. If you go away, you take my happiness with you,"—and the strong man's voice almost broke;—"but even you, dearly beloved, cannot take away the desire to make of my life all that God intended I should make of it."

As he ceased speaking, Elsa stepped back and cried, "Indeed! I am not half

as good as you would make me out. I
went to Mrs. Leadbetter's because I
needed the money ; believe me, that was
my principal motive." And into the eyes
of the surprised and over-wrought girl
rushed the quick tears.

"I do not think you faultless," he
replied gently. "That being the case, I
should not want you for myself ; you
would make me appear in too bad a light.
But I need you ; I want you !" The
words were spoken with an intensity and
force that revealed the depth to which
this man's strong nature had been
stirred.

No one could have listened unmoved
to the passionate appeal ; much less the
girl to whom it was addressed. But cau-
tiousness was innate in Elsa's character.
Not only her own happiness, but that of
another was involved ; and while in her

heart she knew there existed not the love this man would claim, was it justice to him, or to herself, to answer, without a careful analysis of her own feelings, this all-important question he had asked of her?

With a sweet dignity Elsa moved away from the man who had drawn near in his fervor, and said: "Mr. Butler, this evening you have paid me the highest compliment a man can pay a woman. It has come most unexpectedly. I should not answer you lightly,—I cannot. You must give me time in which to know myself."

With this decision Donald was forced to be content.

He had not long to wait.

The next evening Elsa slipped this note into the Post Office:

"Somewhere, in my early girlhood, I read these words: 'To love means to think of, to care for, to hope for, and to pray for.' I have always felt, rather than said, that such love as this would I give the man to whom I intrusted my future happiness. At present I have not this affection for you; but my regard can easily ripen into such love. And why? Yours is a nature that would put forth every effort of heart, and brain, and hand, to shield, to solace, and to provide for the woman you love; asking only in return a heart's measure of love, the daily striving to grow 'onward and upward,' and the fulfillment of those womanly duties which alone can make the true home. I feel that you will come to me soon.   ELSA WALTON."

Donald Butler read this message carefully—once, twice. The trusting, confident words stirred him as nothing else could have done. His heart filled to overflowing with the divine passion that, in its purity, humility, and intensity, was Christlike.

"With God's help, I'll not be found wanting," he said; chest heaving and breath coming in short, quick gasps, with the strength of his emotions.

It was a goodly place in which to register such a vow. The setting sun was shimmering its light upon the purple mountains that encircle so lovingly the Salt River Valley. The roar of the Arizona Fall came faintly from the westward. All around him was the emerald green of vines and trees. Overhead the cloudless blue of the sky, suggestive of future bliss. For pure hearts and perfect love can always make an Eden.

THE END.

www.ingramcontent.com/pod-product-compliance
Lightning Source LLC
Chambersburg PA
CBHW030601270326
41927CB00007B/996